Unaccounted For

ALSO BY PAUL SCOLLAN

Liberty Street Hill (poems, 2010)

Unaccounted For

Poems by

Paul Scollan

Antrim House
Simsbury, Connecticut

Library of Congress Control Number: 2015946472

ISBN: 978-1-936482-94-8

First Edition, 2015

Printed & bound by United Graphics, LLC

Book design by Rennie McQuilkin

Front cover oil on canvas painting by Neil Scollan

Author photograph by Hector DeReza

Antrim House
860.217.0023
AntrimHouse@comcast.net
www.AntrimHouseBooks.com
21 Goodrich Road, Simsbury, CT 06070

To family and friends
for their enthusiastic support

Acknowledgments

Grateful acknowledgment to the editors of the following publications in which certain poems in this volume first appeared, some in earlier versions:

Connecticut Poetry Review: "Mind-Magic"

Hartskill Review: "The Architect"

Mastodon Dentist # 27: "Swan"

Pentimento: "Willy"

Time of Singing: "Mad Molly's Watch"

Again, a special thanks to Rennie McQuilkin for editorial guidance.

Table of Contents

II. IN A FACTORY TOWN

Yellow dust on a bumble
bee's wing,
Gray lights in a woman's
asking eyes,
Red ruins in the changing
sunset embers:
I take you and pile high
the memories.
Death will break her claws
on some I keep.

Carl Sandburg
"Troths"

Unaccounted For

JANUARY DROP-IN

They know to come on in,
that the door's unlocked,
and if I'm not inside,
I'll be out in back,
enlivened by the cold,
doing the daily nothing,
like noting the ivy's progress
on the Norway maple
that hugs the back porch,
or checking to see
if the hornet nest
dangling from the oak branch
weathered the whiplashing
rain-squall the night before,
or maybe eye-balling
the flat sprawling dead
in the garden beds –
only months ago
too alive for me to describe
in fitting detail.

Oh, there you are,
I didn't see you.
Come inside,
there's lots of stories
to tell, old friend –
about the highs,
the lows, or nothing
at all – the nothing

always a big something.
Good to see you.
Sit down
and have a beer
or glass of wine.

I. NET WORTH

EDUCATION

A boy of 12, I'm at the carnival,
first time there alone at night.
I follow the fairway lights
to the fried dough booth
where I'm to meet a girl.
I wait and wait.
She doesn't show up,
so I give up and walk deeper
into the star-domed arcade
of cries on wheels fading in and out,
a calliope waltzing to the leg-swings
of riders on the Ferris wheel and whirl-a-gig,
cotton candy spinning from hands behind glass
that leave a white web on a lady's makeup face.

Heading left to the chance booths, I hear ring-toss man
barking, "Just one easy toss, a quarter on a number"
and "Look, just look at the fluffy stuffed prizes,
yours for the taking, easy as pie."
I toss the rings over legions of bottle necks.
On the third try one bounces high and loops a target.
The hair-greased carney flashes a gold tooth
through bobbing cigarette ember, hands me
a stuffed elephant, a dwarfed version
of the ones on display, this one a frail beast
wrapped in a tissue-thin membrane,
a grimy thumbprint on its head, spilling cotton
from a split seam on the left ear.
I go back and ask for another.

Ring-toss man snickers as he turns
to his busty blonde helper in a halter top,
whacks her bottom as if a prompt for saying,
"Boy, fer notha quarta toss, ya just maht git one."

HERO WORSHIP

I look out over the room
and there he is,
sitting at the corner table
at our 50th reunion,
once the twelve-year-old
whose uncanny curve ball
nicked the corner of the plate
almost every time before
smacking my catcher's mitt,
the pitch that single-handedly
snatched the title for our team.

In dreams and idle musings
over the years, I replayed
the pitch in my head:
the wind-up, release, trajectory,
red stitches on a side-roll
in a downward arc to the batter's
short-reaching swing –
the perfect *true-ness* of it
inspired me over time to dig in deep,
to hone fine edges, focus hard
on every task undertaken thereafter.

After the hand-shaking, back-slapping,
cracking wise about the ravages of age,
I cut straight to worshipful words
about the boy wonder on the mound,
enough to enshrine him in Cooperstown.
Boy Wonder hears me out in full

but with puzzlement in his eyes.
He comes back with a dismissive sweep
of the hand, saying, "Thanks, ole buddy,
but you got it all wrong – it was really
the father-and-son coaching duo that won
the day, just in the way they took us in like sons
of their own – making all the difference."

Next day my mind falls back to its usual groove,
but strange to say, the catcher is leaping, lunging,
digging in the dirt to save wild pitches – forgotten
in the stirred-up infield dust of victory day.

TO MY ABDUCTOR

Remember me,
the guy you snatched away
that day in late October,
running errands around town?

Ah, but I remember you,
crouched behind the privet hedge,
with lightning-quick leap
pouncing and snapping me up
by the collar, shaking me silly,
before dragging me over lawns
and woodlots, through a burnt-orange
leaf pile, over soft beds of pine needle
and garden squash gone belly-down,
my legs trailing behind, nose catching
the drift of downwind wood smoke
and wild black grapes hanging low.

At last, heaven knows why,
you set me loose in that lair,
buried in a windfall
beneath a sugar maple,
dazed and face-up to a country
of *yellowness* – leaves like sun-stones
skimming, the blue-enamel sky
spiking me right through the eye.

Next Saturday found me
back there.

COLD CASE

We were 17, Ralphie and I,
just sampling beer for quality,
capacity for quantity.
Our dads snapped into alert status
and showed up to pack us up.

Sobriety came with a thunderclap.
Nothing said between us on the way home.
Stranger still, not a word about it ever after.

His silence slouched in shadow in the back
of my head for decades after he was gone,
till the revelation came in a dream
in which I conducted a cold-case review.

Rummaging through the evidence room,
I dug down deep to find it, a faded brown
folder with a typewritten report inside.
1. Twenty, on a visit with cousin Red
he bar-hopped the Big Apple into the same
hangover with enough concussive impact
to put a powerful aversive notch in his
knuckle-headed brain.
2. His son's guilt-payment: paint porch,
mow lawn, clean the basement…

On the last page was a handwritten note
in my father's hen-scratch that read:
Conclusion – one free pass given.
The knucklehead doesn't deserve it,
but should get one, just like his old man.

LETTER TO A WOULD-BE PACIFIST

1. Bus to Vancouver

They prepared you for your designated
place in the paddies and jungles,
had you fire all the military hardware,
learn the latest methods of warfare,
what to expect from the cunning, tunneling
enemy called gooks aka Charlie Cong,
the black-clad bad guy in the marching song.

Not you, enlightened draftee, you'd
never fall in step to the clang and clash
of armor in a nation gone mad.
You'd hold out, hold on somehow
to your peace credo.

Until the day came.
You rolled out of bed hungover
that off-duty Sunday afternoon,
head aching, muscles aching
from trying to bend your sword
into a ploughshare,
and you must remember, college boy,
hearing the chuffing of the bus rounding
the corner of the army barracks, the bus
you knew would take you to Seattle
in an hour or so, from there a short ride
to Vancouver, Canada.

But you just sat there on your bunk
as your ticket-out rolled to a stop,

clapped doors open, clapped them shut,
and lumbered along into tomorrow,
with your credo in tow.

2. A Pheasant

Of all things, a pheasant –
strutting spangled feathers
in a stubbly field surrounding
a gutted Sherman tank
serving as a training target,
and surely you remember
the bird still hanging
there in your periphery
when you bolted into action
in the mortar pit,
the gunner beside you
setting the firing grids,
and you dropped the round
into the tube anyway,
missing the target by twenty feet
and missing the collateral damage
by a mile, because the *thump*
of the round hitting the bottom
of the tube was Mr. Pheasant's cue
to make a fast wing-beating retreat
from the mangled tank.

But you, sorry to say,
Private Mortar Man,
who'd never hurt a friggin flea,
didn't really know that –
until after the *thump*.

3. The Grenade

So off you go to Vietnam,
to that base camp up north,
a hopeful *Objector* on guard duty,
keeping watch from a bunker
piled high with sandbags,
standing in the pitch-blackness
broken by popping balls of light,
mortar-fired illumination rounds
floating down on tiny parachutes
over rows of razor wire strung deep
on the perimeter, making it easier
to spot an intruder –
but the swaying candles also made
way for a parade of moving shadows
that played tricks on vigilant eyes –
your eyes – and you'd swear you saw
an enemy sapper splayed inside the wire.

You knew it had been placed there,
that grenade.
You reached for it,
wrapped fingers around it,
locked eyes on the sapper's location –
false alarm!

So began the long off-beat patter
inside the head of the wingless dove.

Sorry to bring it up, ole buddy.

STOCKADE FENCE

We were basic trainees,
all draftees, marching
and singing the army cadence
with Drill Sergeant Lopez in the lead,
Vietnam, Vietnam, late at night
while you're sleeping Charlie
Cong comes a-creeping around,
to an old pop tune, "Poison Ivy."

After a day at the firing range
with Charlie in our sights,
we were marching back to barracks
when we passed the stockade's
outer fence in the exercise yard,
with a dozen or so confined soldiers
of every stripe and infraction,
fingers gripping the wire mesh
over heads, faces scrunched
against it, shouting taunts as far
as voice could carry, the likes of
Ya ass-lickin' gung-ho wusses – or,
Hey, sucker, they'll send your sorry
asses home in a plastic sandwich bag.

But we the trainees on the fence's other
side kept marching, marching in cadence
to our destiny past the fenced-in chorus,
till the heckling was drowned out
by our marching feet and the cadence

sounding out in synchronized beat –

… while you're sleeping Charlie
Cong comes a-creeping around.

BUCK PRIVATE DANNY, 1969

Through it all, through basic's first week of sunup jogs,
classes on military protocol and endless marching drills,
Private Danny pressed the little Bible tightly in his hand,
and when left no choice stuffed it in a pocket.

This scrawny blond kid from a backwater burg in Ohio
hadn't the guile or gall for pretense or malingering –
spoke rarely, smiled benignly, and did all he was asked to do –
which made things dicey for the brass to eject him.

Then came the morning on the firing range. *Cease fire!*
Cease fire! shrieked Sergeant Cruz for all he was worth,
flapping arms like crazy across the firing-line berm
as a body sprinted down-range against bullets flying.

No mistaking it was baby-faced Danny, Bible in hand,
his back to us, racing swiftly to the targets and beyond,
till our boy shrank down to a speck at the wood line,
undeterred in his higher mission – such as it was.

The soldier in Cruz took control, gave orders to our squad
to chase him down, who after all was one of us, and it was
one of us who caught Danny skulking low in the brush,
and brought him back to be handed over.

We the warriors went on to shoot and drill and bivouac
without him, and I would've blotted him out entirely if it
hadn't been for the annoying times I'd hear his timid voice
rising through the *whoooshh-ing* sound of the mortar round.

APPLE-PICKING

Happily trapped in this orchard,
in row after row of apple trees,
all varieties, I took the uphill
footpath flanked by Macouns,
their branches drooping
with clusters of fruit, flawless
in roundness and redness,
a dollop of green here and there
to give a trace of imperfection.
Ahead, at the crest of the hill,
the path dropped off to a caravan
of cumulus, robust and round
as – um, well, a caravan of apples.

On the hilltop I picked my first,
cupped the beauty in my hand
and held it up to the sunlight,
so bedazzling mind and eye
I found myself slipping away
to the first couple holding
this very same apple, and heard
them speaking sweetly back and forth
about what do with it, at last deciding
they would polish the gem for gazing forever
(not yet the mortal scourge of worms, rot,
being bobbed and being candied).

Okay, God, come clean.

MIND-MAGIC

As for walking on air,
I was pretty good at it
when the mood suited
and all the lines met at once
and the sought-after was finally mine.

On tips of pine I'd pivot,
sail and swoop to shame the sparrows,
lighten God's ether, pull the pull of gravity,
high-step the four points of the weathervane,
aerial from the sheer drift of it.

But when the great blow came,
when I really could have used it,
if just as cheap trick or Houdini stunt,
it left me flat, frantic, jamming hands
in every pocket for a simple exit map.

And then the earth opened up,
took the house, the conjugal garden path,
the swing-hung apple tree, still in blossom,
rolled all of it into mauling rock and clay,
myself going down with it, hailing the treetops.

Despite all that, with point-blank stare into my knowing,
I stayed aligned with muscle memory,
breezed my body whole through the drapes and latticework
as the fault-lines webbed along the line of vision,
along the walls and ceiling by the bed

where I tied shoes, knotted ties, made love,
looked into eyes trading slick truths,
saw the blade, felt it running the length of the wall, of me,
yet the *me* they saw held to a painless demeanor.
You must admit, some mind-magic that was!

WOODS OF COULD-HAVE-BEEN

Took off to the woods
of Could-Have-Been — again.
Started out the usual
with purple asters springing
from boulders at my fingers' graze,
fiddlehead ferns waving me on
through mountain laurel
to vernal pools floating lilies
to shame a preening sun,
aspen and hemlock swaying
in welcome to my passing below.

Then next thing I knew, the grid-straight
path looped round to knots,
the ground hung my feet on jagged rock,
maples shook their crowns to fling
tangles of bittersweet vine that stitched
up every portal of sunlight above.

Lost and dazed who knows how long,
I fell into a stream and reached
out to grab a tree limb passing,
hung on for dear life
in those churning waters.

My ride on the life raft slowed
to a drift, came to rest at last
in sandy eddies at the river's bend
shaded by stands of willow and pine,
where a crudely-made sign painted
in red said, *Entering Woods of What-Is.*

AIRBORNE

Leaping arcs through whistling air,
the high-jump skier knows her
hanging skis will touch down first
and meet the angle of the slope.
Digging fingers into tiny nooks
while toeing straight-up walls
with suction feet, the rock-face
climber knows that harnessed rope
and metal loops will catch him
should he slip and fall.

Unprepared for height or flight,
I took swift leave of my back porch
thanks to water over sheets of ice,
and hit the unforgiving walk below.
The in-air pause left hardly chance
to register a thought or feeling,
yet I do recall a flashing picture
of a toddler straying in a crowd,
taking hold of someone's hand –
a hand belonging to a stranger.

GARDEN OF ICE

Was early morning, early January,
the monotony of snow-cover
broken by grassy shoals
here and there across the lawn
after a two-week warm spell.

As I walked out back to take
in the day's offerings,
I spotted a blue-silver geyser
shimmering in sunlight aslant
under the neighbor's pear tree,
its lower limbs laced with icicles,
and, strangely, not the uppers,
and the row of mountain laurel
below took on an aura of glaze.
Moving closer I saw a garden hose
with nozzle upturned, shooting
a fountain of fine mist straight up.

Being neighborly, I turned off
the hose and phoned neighbor Ned,
who swore no one in the household
turned on the hose, convinced it was
some prankster or mischievous vandal
with nothing better to do.
Beauty makes no distinctions,
is what I didn't say.

R&B ON THE RED LINE

In front of me going up the paint-peeled stairway to the
    platform on Roosevelt,
this star-child of twenty years or so was chattering away
    like a birdbath sparrow
in a mixed patois of Iowa plains and South Side Chicago,
and was hanging onto the sleeve of a dark earth-mother,
    salt to pepper,
both going home from work, likely, judging the hour and
    manner of unwinding.
They hopped the same car on the El, landing in a seat
    across the aisle,
star-child rattling on with her mother as the train rattled on.
There was a sweetness, to do with innocence maybe, or close.
She reached for her cell phone and started a three-way
    guessing game
of songs by soul singers she pulled from the past,
    before she was born –
Diana Ross, Gladys Knight, Otis Redding, Fats Domino –
and she crooned so softly, just a few lines as clue,
and there I was, playing along silently, guessing singers
    in my head.

Below me the sprawling city turned brighter and warmer
than I could remember, and as we were rounding The Loop
the lampposts burned a deep orange over the river walk,
    against the LaSalle Bridge,
waving a long banner until the train's sharp turn
    snapped it away,
and my duo got off at Addison, tripping thoughts of
    leave-takings

of my two grown sons down the track, in just a few days,
the same two I left so many times in deference to
    visitation schedules.
Some memories carry an abracadabra penny-trick of
    pain tamped down –
and so reminded, I tucked this one deep into my shoulder bag,
    got off at Berwyn,
and tapped happily under the gray-streaked sky and cold.

TWO OLD DOGS

He's snoozing more,
slower to fetch,
scratching his head a lot,
I've noticed lately,
and what's more, he bumps
into hallway walls looking for
a daydream alcove to snuggle into,
and gnaws on a knuckled bone
while lost in the static passing
through his head these days.

Getting more peculiar, for sure,
these doings of his – he'll be standing
there, just staring at things in the yard,
like the Monarch on the butterfly bush,
wondering aloud how the tiny hairpin
of a body can part the wind and clouds
with its vast fire-inspired parchment,
and the windfall oak, how its small root-ball
can hold a country of catacomb dwellers
who, stunned by the daylight,
crawl warily out of their homes.

I'm worried my master's getting to be
too much like me in his idle musing –
and that can't happen.
It bumps up hard against the order of things.

PAINT PREP

The sun, the planets
and the moon in all phases
fell first, then one by one
the sparkly fill-in stars

fluttered from the ceiling,
those glow-in-the-dark stickers,
touching down only to stick
again to the pile carpet below,

first yielding to my putty knife
scraping the once-white ceiling
of the boys' old bedroom, then
to my fingers teasing them from fiber,

this same night sky put up there by the twin boys
when tall enough to reach the ceiling while standing
on their beds, for lights-out gazing with keychain
flashlights scanning their twelve-year-old cosmos,

now in their mid-thirties, still lifting a glance now
and then, my hope – and I, down there in the celestial
litter on the dingy carpet, pick up and bag the pieces,
except for a few glowing stars that stick to my fingers.

SWEATSHIRT

For my birthday they gave me a sweatshirt,
pointedly meant to replace the old one
and take its space in the dresser drawer
to relegate the old to the household rag factory;
and so out it came
and lay before me on the bed,
face-up to the absurd reluctance
of my gaze on the rumpled relic
with faded-blue tassels from the neck
opening's unstitched collar, cuff
seams forking into snakes' tongues,
a white paint stain the shape of Florida
greeting me from just above the waistband –
a reminder of last July's house trim
and, day's work done, me resting in the grass
as a slender blade of late afternoon sun
drew back through the backyard pines
and over the bed of brick-red pine needles,
passing a few feet from my splayed left leg.
Propping on an elbow, I turned to reach
the burning Excalibur there within my grasp,
but before I could it fled into the squirrel's nest
in the neighbor's maple next door.

The large steel scissors glinted in my hand,
ripped up the length of the seams,
cut swatches of torso in neat square quarters,
dismembered the sleeves into forlorn tubes,
until what remained was a piecemeal shroud,
a useful by-product for spring house painting.

AIDS ALIAS, 1986

His designated alias
was *Tim Olson,*
brother and patient
at that big Boston hospital –
and *Tim Olson*
was the name-key
the lobby's receptionist
gave us, to be sure
we'd locate the right patient.

But before that
we had to give the lady
his real last name,
hoping against hope
the preening of goodness
in our faces
and the eking out of meekness
in our demeanor
would reverse their harsh sentence
and give our brother a reprieve.

JOGGING

No more resolve, just the push of habit;
no more claim to self-discipline,
just falling into sneakers nightly;
and ever so blindly, years
into decades, the route got
shorter, the circle tighter,
twenty-two blocks,
to fifteen, to twelve,
then fewer,
to circles ever-
tightening,
till one day *bam!* he ran
into himself, and flat as jar lids,
he picked *himselves* up, and vowed
then and there to send one to take up kayaking
instead, the other to crank boxes that pop up hidden Jacks.

BIRDS AND BEES

Standing ankle-deep in open
pasture thick with grass and clover,
the old man and little granddaughter
counted the browsing bees
and the pop-up grasshoppers
leaping a high arc over their heads.

Looking straight up she pointed
to a dark broad-winged bird,
watching in awe, unblinking,
as it dipped, soared and tilted
the finger-like tips of its wings
as if directing the flow of clouds.

He reminded her this was
the same creature they spotted
perched on a limb at a rest stop
last summer – a turkey vulture hunched
over with a hard stare, a featherless
blood-raw head and neck and hooked beak –

adding that, being a vulture it feeds
on road-kill and other dead animals as part
of nature's grand plan for all living things,
the earth's cycle of life and death and rebirth.
He paused, pleased at making a teaching point,
doubly pleased to see he had her rapt attention.

Or, she said, maybe he had a beautiful head once,
with a high kingly crown of shiny black feathers –

until God took it away as punishment for thinking
he could do much better at the boring job
of holding sky and clouds and earth together,
and cleaning up the messy litter we make below.

CHESTNUTVILLE

Turning the corner my brothers and I
entered the long semi-dark archway
of chestnut trees along a tucked-away
street of big houses with wide porches,
where the sun of October made very few
passes through the tent of dense floppy leaves;
chestnuts everywhere you looked,
some still in their pulpy green husks,
some as polished-brown nuts peeking
out of husks, others flattened by passing cars,
but most of them shucked and ready for the taking,
and we being kids couldn't resist the urge
to pick them up to toss at targets,
at times with aim at one brother or another.

But these flat-sided stones
just begged to be squirreled away –
for the silky-smooth feel to the fingers,
I suppose, or the *clacking* sound they made
in the pocket, so much like the steely marbles
you'd guard with your life.

So, after tossing my share,
I'd fill my pockets to bursting –
until that day I reached down deep
to find them all gone,
gone along with the treed archway street
and the houses with the come-on-in porches.

All buried under the Interstate.

MISSING

Where do the things still missing go?
The ten-speed bike, the gold silk tie.
I know they're all laid out in a row.

One day the egg man didn't show;
we lived his whistle, no cheerful goodbye.
Where do the things still missing go?

The cancelled trip to Idaho,
the other one the port of Shanghai.
I know they're all laid out in a row.

There's love I never got to know –
she couldn't wait, I couldn't wait to die.
Where do the things still missing go?

Funny how a speck of nothing grows –
the egg man's whistle – only God knows why.
I know they're all laid out in a row.

I go to an enchanted solarium, though,
to watch the specks of nothing float by.
Where do the things still missing go?
I know they're all laid out in a row.

NET WORTH

In tailored suits with candy-cane
neckties on bibs of starched white,
two young salesmen strode into the room
with chests out, posture ramrod straight,
right hands loaded to thrust into mine
for a sober round of finance straight-talk.

Life insurance was what I needed,
said one to the other, nodding –
to ease the doddering worried mind.
Just a matter of finding the right fit:
one to plunder before you're under,
or another that ripens gloriously
for loved ones, to be awarded
posthumously.

Before I could beg off
for a pamphlet
they shuffled plans and riffled papers
for me to sign here, there,
then popped the question quick and bold,
"By the way, what's your net worth?"
A short pause – long enough
to let pass a marching brass funeral band.
"Does that include these shoes?"
I asked, pointing to my battered brogans.
Another pause – much longer.

II. IN A FACTORY TOWN

THE BACHELORS

To my mother

He was kneeling in the pew
in front of her, cardboard poking
through holes in his shoe-sole,
the man with the flattop hair
introduced after Mass on the top
of the church steps –
God as witness, meant to be.

In no time at all they found a nest
in a walkup by the factory wall,
babies started tumbling one two three,
falling down to hands most able
and steadied to catch a fumbling brood –
then, wouldn't you know,
her hands began to crack and bleed,
no way to stop the weeping.

On the evening doorstep, her bachelor
standing with shoulders slumping down,
she heard a crack overhead
as ceilings started to buckle and fall,
rain down plaster on linoleum floors –
sending her fleeing to Bachelor #2.

In the home where they go to count the days,
she babbled to Bachelor #2, waking and sleeping –
'til the man in the picture on her dresser top
started trading faces with the other:

his beard disappeared; his rabbi locks
were clipped back to a flattop,
and if she hadn't known better,
she'd have sworn she was seeing himself
right there at the foot of the stairs,
his shoulders straighter than the evening door jamb,
arms stretched wider than the neighborhood.

WRITING ON THE WALL

Bunch of buddies in their thirties
going back long as memory serves
huddled together at pit-stops
home, off-duty from second lives
of carried cargo –

together again minus one,
their Boy snatched fast
and clean, no final "bye guys,"
no last rascal grin;
the thunderclap of a steel door
slamming
was all they heard;
the flash-pain of branched
lightning over a stopped heart
was all they felt.

How they tried – hung Number 15
jersey over the bar at the watering hole
as second-skin for incarnation
and luck, and with luck enough
the sparks would arc back
and flicker Number 15 forever
on the left field scoreboard screen.

WILLY

Wouldn't be the shy soft-spoken Willy
who kept the books at the bearing factory,
but the other one, the brain-sick Willy
off meds, who slammed dad's hand
in the front door of the house they built,
hammer to nail, buddies in sweat,
he was now dismantling wire by wire
through holes in the drywall, sockets
forlorn in their hanging, nothing unexplored
in his hunt for bugs and wiretaps planted
in nooks by enemies unknown to you and me.

Rubbing his sore hand, his father, a barrel-chested,
hot-tempered Pole stumbled his way to the curb
where I, shrink-rescuer, stood helpless
watching him fall to sitting on the car bumper
and shouting in heavy accent to all that was sacred,
"And me making it through the German camps –
and I can't even save my good boy Willy, my good
son Willy."

And the large callused hands turned to pebbles
that couldn't begin to cover his eyes.

SORE SPORT

The Hobart boys, brothers three,
little leaguers on the same team,
lined up in their driveway after
the two-run loss as their dad
and coach gave his home-front
debriefing, yelling at them
through the part of his mouth
that wasn't cigar to call them out
on the wild pitch, the bobbled
grounder, the unauthorized bunt.
The two older ones held back tears
by scrunching up their faces;
the youngest dropped his cap for cover.
Thank goodness they got most of it
out of their systems at the ball park –
bat slammed against the dugout,
glove thrown over the backstop,
expletives shouted for all to hear.

Years passed, sons gone on to teens
who got to know a thing or three:
how to steal bases from coach-dad,
flick ashes in his face, mock his purpose,
side-step the rules with graceful finesse
or crash head-first with fearless bravado –
the old man no match now for his nimble sons.

There he was, the post-career coach
sitting on his porch, taking a break
on a hot summer afternoon, the lawn

half-cut, the mower leaning sideways,
a slump in his shoulders, the cigar
unlit between limp fingers,
a long head of ash about to fall.

OLD MAN PASTORE'S COLLECTION

Afternoons he'd sit on the oak-shaded
park bench with his loaf of bread,
slowly plucking little pieces to toss
to the squirrels, chipmunks and pigeons,
calling each by its Italian name.

Wasn't long before he started putting off
going home, staying out later and later,
past dark, to watch the kids play soccer
under the lights, and after lights went out,
he'd look for Orion's Sword in the night sky.

On getting word, his only child Vincente
booked the next flight for Scranton,
leaving legal briefs and dockets behind,
and made arrangements on his mobile while
driving to the airport and waiting for his plane.

At the old homestead he did a quick tour
inside and out, noting the effects of neglect
since mother died, and, oh God,
Pop's prized snuff-box collection, too,
once neatly stored on custom shelving,
the more precious ones showcased in glass –

coffin-like boxes of carved teakwood, silver,
inlaid mother-of-pearl, all smaller than his thumb –
now scattered about in disarray, some lids open,
snuff powder spilling over edges, the catalogue
out of sequence, many piling up in the corner.

Taken aback, Vincente fell into Pop's stuffed
chair, doing all he could to gather his senses –
yet still he heard the rise and fall of breathing,
saw shoulders hunched, a bald pate nodding
over knotted fingers barely moving,
and the worried look of a keeper not keeping up
with too many little ones in his care.

MAD MOLLY'S WATCH

She'd call them *lapses,*
those moments when the Old Man nodded,
and this wasn't just anyone dozing off –
this was God she was talking about,
and, yes, she knew you'd say he couldn't be God
if given to such mortal flaws,
but, though strange and silly the notion,
she'd say he was sleeping on the job.
In the beginning, it was nano-seconds,
then, ever so slowly, ever so slightly,
efficiency started slipping, matters left untended:
the scatter of adversity meant to strengthen character
became grand, sweeping natural disasters.
The Plan got away from him,
even the Great Flood got out of hand –
too big, too apocalyptic, too Cecil B. deMille-ish.
While tugging on a smoke with tremulous hand,
she'd tell all who would listen
how one day the Old Man came to her
in a whisper from lips grazing her ear.
One small favor, he asked, just one –
that she keep him from dozing,
and she'd know it was coming
by the itch near the birthmark on her ankle.
With all her might she must train her focus
on the tiny hairs residing in his nose,
enough to make him sneeze and rouse him.

And that's what she did, for a time,
but the pressure got to be too much,

and soon she cracked under the strain,
waking up in the psych ward one morning,
dribbling pills. No more birthmark itch,
no more keeping watch,
no more whisperings from the Old Man –
except years later, the last time.

The message seemed clear at first,
saying her work was done,
and he was ever so grateful.
She was never entirely sure
of the words that followed.
She thought she heard him say,
"Now we are tumbling toward the night,"
and at other times,
"Now we are fumbling for the light."

SWAN

I could swear
her eyes glistened
as she started telling
the story of the swan
flying low over the bridge
she crossed that morning,
how a wing glanced the top
of the tractor-trailer cab
in front of her, went hurling down
to a sprawl across two lanes,
a peculiar whiteness widening,
neck curved to a question mark,
wings clasped in prayer
to passing cars in their racing pace.

Her voice, it grew husky and cracked,
breathing stopped.
In a blink, the discomposure
powdered over, and with a flutter
of her dragon-lady lashes
she gathered up her swagger,
snapped back to tattooed Lulu,
the lady I knew so well
in the vale-of-tears room
where I did my armchair voodoo.

Lulu was back,
and Lulu blurted,
"That dumb-ass bird
needed a co-pilot – me."

PURGATORY

Nina couldn't say no.
It was dear friend Hilda
asking her to go.

So, together they sat in the monastic chapel
with a few dozen others beside and behind them
in the pinewood pews, mostly older widow types
with heads covered, and a few stone-faced men.
As Nina's mind skimmed the shallows
of regret for giving in to the invitation,
a muffin-faced nun in starched habit strode down
the aisle through stained-glass cascades of yellows
and blues and reds cast over the baptismal font
and the backs of pews – and stood before them.

Sister Anna lectured on faith and doctrine –
on sin (original, venial, mortal, cardinal and deadly),
on indulgences (partial and plenary),
the concept of Limbo (just recently "rescinded"),
the afterlife of Heaven, Hell and Purgatory,
the latter sketched as some drab windowless
waiting room for the not-quite-ready souls
holding out in anguish for their names to be called.
Not one to hold back, Nina threw up her hand, blurting,

"Sister, pardon me, I'm emotional, I'm Italian –
but why not rescind Purgatory, too?
Haven't we suffered enough, suffered enough in this life?"

A few throat-clearings followed – then utter silence.

At the break for a soup-and-sandwich buffet,
they filed patiently for the meager luncheon fare.
Sister carried an extra soup bowl to the table,
after propping her briefcase on the chair beside her –
to save a place for Our Lady of Rescind.

FATS

On piano scales, diligent;
on three assigned polonaises, diligent.
Under the delicate glass dome
of Chopin she found bliss,
for a time –
then all of that changed
on hearing the man on the radio,
the wizard of the ivory-striding fingers
and the high hallelujah of the vocal pipes.
It was Thomas Wright Waller,
i.e. Fats – love at first listen.
To piano tutor Miss Adams this
was pure frivolity and distraction –
musically misbehavin', she said,
pleased as punch with her word play.

She wouldn't stop pestering Miss Adams
to play him, though, and it paid off:
her ruler-wielding mentor caved in
at last, but not without conditions,
mind you – only if the next lesson
were completed to her satisfaction,
and only a few bars.

Next week, with hands poised over the keys,
hands detached from the inert rest of her,
posture ramrod straight on the bench,
Anna Lee Adams dipped her fingers,
lightly at first, into *Honeysuckle Rose,*
and before you knew it, she dove

into it body and soul, her young student
there beside her wrapped in its rapture,
who, in her eighties umpteen years later,
stuck to her story – that Miss Adams'
buttocks started bouncing on the bench,
shoulders rolling along in rhythm,
a half-smile creeping over her face,
then quickly suppressed.

DOCTORATE

If they had an honorary
doctorate in Mother Wit
she'd be the one
to get it,
forget her only sheepskin
was a high school diploma
from a sharecropper schoolhouse
in red-clay gravel-road Georgia,
land of landless field hands.

A shame she was passed up
for Mental Health Aide Two,
for truth to tell
she could read body cues,
sniff out hurt and anguish
better than any sleuth of inner life,
pedigreed shrinks to boot.

In no time she'd have
a kicking mule licking her hand,
such were her healing ways
to those within her far-reaching reach.

And that was enough
for her, for them, for us.
Shame.

MILLER'S AND THE GOLDEN SPIKE

Most of the factories are gone now,
the oil-stained workers too, so many of them
regulars once at Miller's after whistle blow,
but wouldn't you know, the watering hole
still stands and runs in its closet of a barroom,
now sandwiched between a wig shop and dollar store
but looking pretty much the same inside and out –
the same propped sandwich-board sign luring
the thirsty with a badly painted pitcher of beer,
the worn floorboards sagging low at the center,
the polished bar abutting the front window
looking out on the weedy sidewalk and the street –

which is where you'll find Cadge, the keeper
of memory, sitting any weekday afternoon
with his left elbow against the softball trophy,
holding court with the barkeep and two buddies,
and checking the passing trains now and then.

Then there's the day Cadge started babbling
on and on about an omen that came to him
in the shape of a golden rail spike of sunlight
forking through the batter's arms on the trophy,
striking the wall clock over the bar and the amber
bottle of beer in his hand, nearly blinding him.

Something held him captive thereafter,
some warm tingly feeling inside, much warmer
than the glow of good whiskey going down.
Then the buzz of bar chatter started slowing

down to the flow of honey on a flat table,
and the barbs he heard had no reach to his heart,
even with the teasing about the golden spike.

The train rumbled in. Cadge checked his watch.
Right on time. He got up, walked out the door
to the weed-fringed walk and the whistle.

GINNY DOA

In one continuous flow
she moved from quilted bed
to flannel robe to slippers,
skating on the kitchen tile
to finger on the coffee switch.

Waiting for the pot to brew
she spread her girth into the chair
next to the kitchen window
and watched a squirrel jump
on top of the gnome lawn ornament
and drop down in a scurry
under her trailer home.

Alone but holding her own
she poured herself a cup,
wrapped hands around the curves
and took a sip, feeling the warmth
move down her belly and up to her chest,
holding a glow she'd never known.

She heard the sunlight trickling
in through the curtain ruffles,
heard the lilac buds bursting
fast against the dew-streaked glass,
heard the whirring of the unspooling
maple leaves buried deep inside
the branch shoots outside the window.

Strange to feel so different now,
fear and rage and jealousy
so suddenly dissolved,
those mock-companions seducing
her oh so many years.
Now she only felt a calm, the kind
that comes with unburdening.

Ginny watched the squirrel perch
on top of the garden gnome – again,
but this time it stood straight and tall
on its hind legs and looked into her eyes,
and she could tell it knew her.

PAVING STONE

Was a paving stone stepped on
that twisted her ankle on the walk
to the bus stop, slowing her down
to a hobble and causing her to miss the bus,
leaving no choice but to call in sick,
to be told she'd be let go despite
a good work record, and with that
came the loss of her medical plan,
the lifeline for her out-of-work
husband and autistic son,
thus spiking their debt sky-high,
and before they knew it
two months back rent
and the landlord's final notice
putting them out on the street
to sleep in the beat-up station wagon
and into the hands of social workers
and the kindness of strangers.

Was the same small stone
kicked up over the curb
by a dump truck five years ago,
embedded in the grass strip
between the curb and sidewalk,
then dislodged onto the walk last week
by the neighbor kid on his skateboard,
next day almost brushed back
onto the grass strip by two leashed dogs

crossing paths, one of the dogs belonging
to the bus driver who later wouldn't stop
to wait for the limping waving lady
he saw in his side-view mirror
because he was behind schedule.

THE ARCHITECT

It was Rafe's most daring design,
most detailed blueprint,
the house he hoped to live in one day,
alone, an oval glass dome high on a cliff
over pinnacled pine and spruce,
above a virgin lake in Idaho
where, over morning coffee, he'd see
surfacing trout and gliding hawk shadows
passing over the polished-stone floor.
Evenings he'd sit on his cantilevered shelf of stone,
gazing into the mask of moon on the lake,
and the glass roof would host constellations of stars
he'd trace with his finger till sleep took over.

One Day never came. Forty years later
the dream house had never left paper,
and the only cliff he reached was the one
for dropping straight down in a final swan dive.
He propped himself up, found a cheap
second-story rent in a drive-by factory town,
spending his days sitting on the stairway's last
step to the sidewalk and waving to passersby.
Lying on his bed at night he'd gaze for hours
into his dream-house sketch pinned on the wall,
see himself walking around from room to room,
alone at first, monk-like, till some tilting
of the innermost unpinned him from the wish
for solitude to the need to open the hatch
to greet the sidewalk greeters
who knew nothing about the descent,
to whom the knowing wouldn't matter anyway.

BUICK REGAL

Bumped into Mr. Bergeron
at the coffee shop early morning –
no mistaking that Gallic nose,
short wiry body and jaunty gait.
His story told me in my teens
percolated up on seeing him –
how at age nineteen a landing craft
disgorged him onto an ashen atoll
in the Pacific where he only moved
by crawling on his belly with his buddies,
eating ashen dirt, shitting in his pants
without knowing it, and spitting curses
against every deafening spray of metal.

He grinned a wide grin on seeing me,
threw out a hand for firm shaking,
then waved me out to the parking lot
for a look at his brand-new Buick Regal
sitting there lolling in its imperial shine.
Finishing the tour inside and out,
he paused while leaning against a fender,
dropping word matter-of-factly
as rain on rooftops –
the doctors gave him
but a few months more.

Before I could muster a lame response,
he gave a wink and pat on the back,
tucked the *New York Post* under his arm

as he snatched up his cup of take-out joe
from the hood, then slung himself
into his slick black Buick Regal –
his fourth-to-last time driving it.

A SPIT OF SAND

Beauty, children, choices gone,
the string of men the same, thank God.
Back home from nights of waiting tables,
she props her feet and reads till dozing,
stirs awake at some wee hour
to cast about inside her head
to fetch the scene that's waiting there –
a South Pacific spit of sand,
two palm trees standing by themselves,
a hammock strung between the two.
She's stretched out in the slender pouch,
swinging far to touch the salty wet
on one side and the other,
till waters rise and catch her gently,
wash her clean from birth to Tuesday,
wash her out to sea,
a life ahead of misery.

TALK-BACK MAN

They used to call me Talk-Back Man
for the way I'd shout the voices down
on daily walks around this factory town.
Crazy, they'd say, and so few really knew
I was cursing the sky and my maker
for the demons screaming in my head,
for shrinks and pills that made them louder,
for kids who mimicked me *just because,*
guests patronizing at family gatherings.

One blustery day an oak limb snapped
and fell on my head as I turned on Broad,
bringing down a curse with a blessing
following close behind.
Doctors stitched the gash in my head,
said I'd be fine and sent me home –
and how right they were,
for the demons fled, never to return.
From that day on, no more shaking
fists at the sky – only folding them
in thankful deliverance.

No more deafening rattle of tin cans rolling
nor the ear-burst of church bell's tolling,
no wild-eyed pitches from the shrinks
claiming the latest miracle potion,
no off-key squeal from the devil's fiddle
leading me down to turbulent waters.

Now it's a strange silence

and the softest humming that comes
with a warm hand on my heart.

Now when I look above the tips
of cedar, spruce and pine,
I see a swarm of circling stars
that dance around my head
and get my feet to dancing.

TOO MUCH COINCIDENCE

He knew he wasn't dead
on realizing the luminous celestial
aura was really an overhead
dome with a metal frame around it,
and the radiant persona beckoning
him through the clouds
was the pocked, bearded face
of a paramedic adjusting his oxygen mask
in a silence broken only by a siren's wail.

Everything had gone according to plan:
he'd parked on the gravel road in the woods
before the sun came up, hooked up the hose
to the exhaust, run it through the window,
making sure the opening around the hose
was sealed, the engine would idle softly
as he drifted off to Rachmaninoff on his CD,
no one left to miss him but his ex-wife
and creditors – only for the payment stoppage.

Released from the hospital's psych unit,
he was assigned to me for follow-up care,
the "psychotherapist" who'd hoist him up
from the well of despair, pump up his deflated
hope and shriveled opinion of himself –
but no need for all that, for our patient
had already arrived.

"What're the odds a construction worker'd show
on his way to a work site?" he kept saying

over and over, as if hearing the news the first time.
"Too much coincidence to not have a reason" –
last words on his first and last talking session,
which he left before his time was up.

FIFTEEN-MINUTE MASS

Saying Mass in rapid-fire Latin
in fifteen minutes was more habit
than anything else as this had been
Father McBride's drill as chaplain
on the deck of his battleship in WWII –
short and sweet for safety's sake –
though taxing on us the altar boys
who couldn't fire back fast enough.

Some Masses were even shorter,
those mornings when the shrapnel
wound to his throat would act up,
sending him into fits of coughing
and a sputtering apology
about having to cancel the sermon.

When he did step up to the pulpit,
it was Gospel According to McBride,
putting Jesus, Peter, John, Thomas,
James and the others right in front
of you so you could smell their sweat,
see the dirt-caked sandaled feet kicking
up dust, feel the hot Judean sun, hear small
talk about weather, wives, family, the risky
venture with the traveling ministry tour,
see Bethany village's row of sunken houses,
hear the creaking donkey carts, the buzzing flies,
the haggling chatter in the open market.

Because the story's telling was his, you might
also see some of the twelve as sailors on liberty
stopping for a beer at a gin mill to let loose
and bitch about the ship's commander and all
the others who outranked them – yet hop ship
and go back out to sea anyway,
and as alarms sounded, scuttle up on deck
for whatever surprises awaited.

LITTLE HOME ON WHEELS

The motorized scooter comes trundling downhill
in the drizzle, hitting each sidewalk crack
with a thump, not a blink from the driver
in trench coat, wrapped scarf and floppy hat,
as the oversized fastened umbrella shakes wildly,
sending spasms of rain droplets all around her.
Her poodle sits up in a box on the foot stand,
ears perked and, if dogs can smile, is smiling.
The handlebars sport a boxy radio,
a squeeze-bulb horn and a Red Sox pennant
beating madly against her forearm
and in the rear, a small cargo flatbed holding
a wooden crate overflowing with filled
shopping bags, a bicycle pump, a baseball
bat – for protection, perhaps – and God
only knows what else.

My guess, she is forty or so.
So many times I've seen her come and go.
Her stubby legs dangle like a ventriloquist
dummy's – which is where the simile stops,
for I'll bet there's no hand or thrown voice
to steer this Windwagon Smith of the sidewalk,
no legs to stand on needed,
no help or good intentions wanted,
no home more complete (and it moves, no less),
than this lady's little world on wheels.

ORANGE CREAMSICLE

What an ice cream
truck it is –
large and boxy,
wedding-gown white,
lording over the city
block like a Presbyterian
chapel on wheels,
with a driver's cab
high off the curb, giving
an upper-story view of
curbs standing in dandelions
and heads bobbing
a whole street ahead.
Big side-view mirrors
catch kiddy sprinters
windmilling from behind
in a dance of desperation
to the tinkly tones
of a Disney tune.

No ringing bells of days past,
no white-uniformed man
with a silvery gadget on his belt
coughing out coins for change –
instead, this is a black-eyed lady
in a flowery dress cascading
over her feet on the pedals
and crowned with an orange headscarf,
deep and delicious to the eye.

An orange creamsicle floats
through the truck's side window
to a small upturned hand
and mouth open for bitefuls –
but it still pales to bland and melts
undelightful next to the orange
headscarf reaching to the shoulders
of our black-eyed lady.

APRIL TOUR, FACTORY TOWN

Above me, a half-painted steeple on a drop-cloth of indigo;
over there, Jake's barber pole turning spirals in a puddle;
beyond, the all-night diner giddy with sunlight on its chrome.

Here, no mists rolling off the Adirondacks,
no clipper masts parting clouds in Mystic Port,
no million glowing windows from towers looking down.

This town's content with shade-tree mechanics, plaid flannel,
liver spots, bird-nest hair, front porches for sitting,
elder strollers tapping canes on uneven slate walks.

It's an old suit vest without the suit, with orphaned buttons
that don't match –
and when one pops off lost, you'll see me looking.

FOURTH OF JULY, FACTORY TOWN

Walking downtown, downhill
all the way, I see scattered stands
of weed-tree squatter Ailanthus
flagging me down from side-street curbs
and along the crooked factory fence,
its leaf-fingers high-fiving me as I pass
by, brushing my elbow to beg a ride
on my shoulder or in my back pocket,
welcome to come along on this evening fest
of shooting stars whistling to a *crack.*

There's living alive and thriving to be found
in smoke-trails coming from multifamilies
in family cookout scenes in shaded nooks,
grottos of flagstone patio, back-porch stoops,
postage-stamp yards ringed with folding chairs,
kids toeing soccer balls, volley ball nets buckling,
netless hoops banging and rattling apace
with friendly taunts and jeers from old folks
fanning cards in small huddles – all syncopated
with sounds of reggae, samba, Ella's blues, salsa,
Caribbean steel drums, Willy's river of whiskey,
and the smells of barbecuing meats to trump all else
on this evening fest of stars, all shooting stars
exploding overhead.

I walk back up the hill and see Ailanthus,
tree of paradise, bending, waving, standing
tall, saying to all, *Here I am.*

HANDY'S _ARDWARE

Full moon and evening
star hung frozen over
the missing *H* sign
on Handy's _ardware
seen from the third booth
in Al's all-night diner
that early morning
is what I see in twilight sleep
just before falling –
only difference being
there's no *H* missing.

TORRANCE TERRACE

A late-afternoon October walk,
last glance over the shoulder,
I feel again the pull
to round the bend to queerly
lovely Torrance Terrace.
Torrance for the long-gone corner pub
second home to hard-knuckled
workers at whistle-blow,
Terrace tacked on by a visored clerk
with a fancy for felicitous rhyme.

The half-circle lane sits in a thicket
of a dozen rambling multifamilies
huddled together shoulder to shoulder,
porches sagging, screen doors flapping
loud in the wake of kids on a skitter,
a sun-bleached shutter turning to a tilt.
A bird-flocked statue of St. Francis
Assisi peeks over the overrunning goldenrod
to a strip of fresh-cropped lawn
with a corner niche of white ceramic-like
roses spiraling up a trellis.

As the parting sun peels back
the unpruned hedges and dormers,
I stop to catch the evening's torch song
in this humble side-road, to me a busy someplace –
in the gilded medallion on a window shade,

in the long dragging shadows of light poles
and tree limbs slipping over the stone birds
of St. Francis, the swing-door porch, the tangled
white roses on the trellis top, aiming
for a passing wisp of cloud from nowhere.

WEST-SIDE WINDOW

I feel this tugging pull
to walk outside on evenings
when the sun tilts low
and ducks behind brick
storefronts, parked cars,
leaning fences and linden
trees standing in a line,
winking at me
in my passing periphery,
and I get to see the house
with the wrapped porch
as wide and welcoming
as an old aunt's Sunday hug,
with two wicker rockers
by the old oak doors,
tilting with the lightest
graze of a passing breeze.

I slow down to a shuffle
by the west-side window
as shadows break
through the fluttery maple,
throwing stencil patterns
against the clapboards,
and the last strands of sunlight
pull away from the white lace
curtains in the parlor window
and hang a breath or two
on top of the high-back chair
and slip through the floor-lamp

shade before dragging
a fingernail along the window
sash – and then the long sigh
of hesitation, slow and aching,
when I have to go on walking.

FACTORY TOWN

So say some people, people in the know,
it's the over-grown kid gone wrong
that only a mother could love.

I see a back-street lot all crazed with cracked tar,
as well a Wordsworth's meadow of thistle
and chicory in a drunk's sway of standing
purple all the way to the loading dock and back,
a brick-faced corridor burning the eye,
as well the parting sun's backboard mural
of last-minute sketches of beauty unexpected,
a row of windows from a soot-smudged eave,
as well the image-keepers of cupolas and steeples,
of haystack clouds tagging one after the other.

ABOUT THE AUTHOR

Paul Scollan recently retired after more than thirty-five years as a clinical social worker and administrator at mental health centers. His poetry has its source in his professional work, his years of travel in Spanish-speaking countries, his experience in the Vietnam War, and the wonderful peculiarities of being from a large Irish-Catholic family. His first book, *Liberty Street Hill,* was published in 2010 and was a finalist for the Eric Hoffer Award in 2012. His poems have have appeared in many journals including *The Connecticut River Review, Sow's Ear, The William and Mary Review,* and *Oasis Journal.* They pay homage to the unnoticed, avoided and unsung, look for beauty, mystery and spirituality in the most unlikely places, and strive for honesty, though painful at times, in telling of his personal past. A native son of Connecticut, Paul lives in Meriden.

This book is set in Garamond Premier Pro, which had its genesis in 1988 when type-designer Robert Slimbach visited the Plantin-Moretus Museum in Antwerp, Belgium, to study its collection of Claude Garamond's metal punches and typefaces. During the mid-fifteen hundreds, Garamond—a Parisian punch-cutter—produced a refined array of book types that combined an unprecedented degree of balance and elegance, for centuries standing as the pinnacle of beauty and practicality in type-founding. Slimbach has created an entirely new interpretation based on Garamond's designs and on compatible italics cut by Robert Granjon, Garamond's contemporary. Titles are set in Perpetua Titling, a variant of the font designed by Eric Gill, whose work as a stone mason led to the clean lines of Perpetua.

To order additional copies of this book
or other Antrim House titles, contact the publisher at

Antrim House
21 Goodrich Rd., Simsbury, CT 06070
860.217.0023, AntrimHouse@comcast.net
or the house website (www.AntrimHouseBooks.com).

•

On the house website
in addition to information on books
you will find sample poems, upcoming events,
and a "seminar room" featuring supplemental biography,
notes, images, poems, reviews, and
writing suggestions.